MW00427063

A COWBOY'S GUIDE TO LIFE

THE QUOTATIONS IN THIS BOOK COME FROM A MIXTURE OF LORE AND EXPERIENCE.

A COWBOY'S GUIDE TO LIFE

TEXAS BIX BENDER

GIBBS SMITH
TO ENRICH AND INSPIRE HUMANKIND

THE COWBOY CODE

In sun and shade, be sure by your friends.

Never swing a mean loop.

Never do dirt to man or animal.

There never was a horse that couldn't be rode; there never was a man that couldn't be throwed.

NEVER INTERFERE WITH SOMETHING THAT AIN'T BOTHERIN' YOU NONE.

TIMING HAS A LOT TO DO WITH THE OUTCOME OF A RAIN DANCE.

IF YOU'RE
CARRYING A BIG
ROLL, DRESS
DOWN, NOT UP.

THERE IS NEVER A SHORTAGE OF
GOOD HORSE SENSE ON THIS PLANET.

OF COURSE, IT'S MOSTLY THE
HORSES THAT HAVE IT.

A good pard will
ride with you
till hell freezes
over—and a little
while on the ice.

**Every quarrel
is a private one.
Outsiders are
never welcome.**

THERE'S NO USE FOR A MAN WHO OWNS A DOG TO DO THE BARKING HIMSELF.

AFTER WEEKS OF BEANS AND TATERS, EVEN A CHANGE TO TATERS AND BEANS IS GOOD.

NEVER TAKE TO SAWIN' ON THE BRANCH THAT'S SUPPORTIN' YOU,

UNLESS YOU'RE BEIN' HUNG FROM IT.

NEVER KICK A FRESH TURD ON A HOT DAY.

After eating an entire bull, a mountain lion felt so good he started roaring. He kept it up until a hunter came along and shot him. The moral: when you're full of bull, keep your mouth shut.

If you find yourself
in a hole, the
first thing to do is
stop diggin'.

THE EASIEST WAY TO EAT CROW
IS WHILE IT'S STILL WARM.
THE COLDER IT GETS,
THE HARDER IT IS TO SWALLER.

ENJOY BEING YOURSELF, WHATEVER THAT IS.

YOU CAN'T TELL HOW FAR A FROG CAN JUMP BY HIS CROAK.

Beware the pessimist—the sort of hombre who hangs around the train depot and tells everybody the train is never gonna get here. When it chugs into view, he says, They'll never get that thing stopped. When it stops, he says, Uh huh, they'll never get it started again. When it fires up and heads off, he says, Well, that's the last we'll ever see of that thing.

WHETHER THE GLASS IS HALF EMPTY OR HALF FULL DEPENDS ON WHETHER YOU'RE DRINKIN' OR POURIN'.

Be careful about sayin' "it can't be done." Somebody's liable to interrupt you by doin' it.

BEFORE YOU LET ANYBODY MEASURE
YOU FOR THE BIG WOODEN OVERCOAT,
MAKE SURE YOU'VE WRUNG ALL THE
LIFE OUT OF YOUR LIVIN'.

IF YOU'RE ITCHIN' TO HAVE SOMETHIN', YOU'D BETTER BE READY TO SCRATCH FOR IT.

A Texas breakfast is a two-pound
hunk of steak, a quart of whiskey,
and a hound dog. If you're
wondering why you need the dog—
well, somebody has to eat the steak.

Grumbling makes
you about as
welcome as a
sidewinder in
a cow camp.

IT DON'T TAKE A GENIUS
TO SPOT A GOAT IN A
FLOCK OF SHEEP.

WHEN DEALIN'
WITH A SLICK
SON OF A BITCH,
START OFF BY
PINNIN' HIM
DOWN AND
CHANGIN' HIS OIL.

29

The good thing about cowboyin' is that any boss will gladly give you 18 hours to do your day's work.

If you find you're drinkin' most of
your entertainment out of a can, it's
time to look for your fun elsewhere.

THERE'S A HIGH COST TO LOW LIVING.

THE BIGGEST LIAR YOU'LL EVER
HAVE TO DEAL WITH PROBABLY
WATCHES YOU SHAVE HIS FACE
IN THE MIRROR EVERY MORNING.

IF YOUR GUTS
HAVE TURNED
TO FIDDLE
STRINGS ON THE
COWBOY TRAIL,
IT AIN'T GOOD FOR
YOU AND IT AIN'T
SAFE FOR ME.

IF YOU GET TO THINKIN' YOU'RE A PERSON OF SOME INFLUENCE,

TRY ORDERIN' SOMEBODY ELSE'S DOG AROUND.

Never try to
run a bluff
when your
poke's empty.

If at first you don't
succeed, try to hide
your astonishment.

IF YOU'VE GOT A VOICE LIKE A
BURRO WITH A BAD COLD—THE KIND
THAT MAKES A COYOTE CRINGE—
DON'T RISK SINGIN' TO THE HERD.

TALK LOW, TALK SLOW, AND DON'T SAY TOO MUCH.

Never believe
anybody who
says their horse
doesn't kick.

GIVEN THE RIGHT
DOSE OF PRICKLY
PEAR, ANY NAG
WILL BUCK.

SORRY LOOKS BACK.

WORRY LOOKS AROUND.

FAITH LOOKS UP.

A SMART ASS
JUST DON'T FIT
IN A SADDLE.

NO MATTER WHO
SAYS WHAT,
DON'T BELIEVE IT
IF IT DON'T
MAKE SENSE.

A man with an edgy smile is
like a dog with a waggin' tail:
he's not happy; he's nervous.

DON'T WORRY ABOUT BITING OFF
MORE THAN YOU CAN CHEW.

YOUR MOUTH IS PROBABLY A
WHOLE LOT BIGGER 'N YOU THINK.

Going faster
when you're
lost won't
help a bit.

SOFT GRUB, FEATHER BEDS, AND EASY LIVIN' CAN LEAD TO A SOLD SADDLE.

If there's a hole in your story or your fence, whatever you'd rather didn't get out . . . will.

GOOD JUDGMENT
COMES FROM
EXPERIENCE—
AND A LOT OF
THAT COMES
FROM BAD
JUDGMENT.

Always drink upstream from the herd.

"LOOK OUT" USUALLY MEANS "DON'T LOOK—DUCK!"

NEVER BLUFF WHEN YOU'RE DEALING WITH A WOMAN.

YOU'RE NOT BEING DIPLOMATIC
JUST BECAUSE YOU PUT "PLEASE"
IN FRONT OF "SHUT THE HELL UP!"

Generally, you ain't
learnin' nothin'
when your mouth
is a-jawin'.

TELLIN' A MAN TO GO TO HELL AND MAKIN' HIM DO IT ARE TWO ENTIRELY DIFFERENT PROPOSITIONS.

THE PUREST METAL COMES OUT OF THE GREATEST HEAT.

IF THE JOB YOU DID SPEAKS FOR ITSELF . . .

★ ★ ★

DON'T INTERRUPT.

ONE GOOD THING ABOUT BEING A COWBOY IS THAT YOU JUST DON'T HAVE TIME FOR GOLF.

WHEN YOU'RE IN THE WRONG
AND YOU NEED TO SET IT RIGHT,
HOW FAR YOU HAVE TO TRAVEL
IN THE DOIN' OF IT HAS NOTHING
TO DO WITH THE RIGHTIN' OF IT.

Makin' it in life is
kinda like bustin' broncs:
You're gonna get thrown a lot.

The simple secret is to
keep gettin' back on.

IT'S ALWAYS A BIT CONFUSING WHEN SOMETHIN' GOES RIGHT.

NEVER MISS A CHANCE TO REST YOUR HORSE.

A SUBTLE JOKE
ABOUT A MAN'S
CHARACTER
CAN RUIN A
REPUTATION
FASTER THAN
AN OBVIOUS LIE.

THE BEST WAY TO COOK ANY
PART OF A RANGY OL' LONGHORN
IS TO TOSS IT IN A POT WITH
A HORSESHOE, AND WHEN THE
HORSESHOE IS SOFT AND TENDER,
YOU CAN EAT THE BEEF.

Remain independent
of any source of
income that will
deprive you of your
personal liberties.

GENERALLY SPEAKING,
FANCY TITLES AND
NIGHTSHIRTS ARE
A WASTE OF TIME.

HARD-BOILED EGGS ARE YELLOW AT THE CORE.

Cowboyin' would be a lot more pleasant
if Noah had taken the time to
swat a couple of mosquitoes on his ark.

A hand who's not there when you need him is like a blister— it only shows up when the work's all done.

IF YOU AIN'T PULLIN' YOUR WEIGHT,

YOU'RE PUSHIN' YOUR LUCK.

WHEN A RUNNING HORSE GETS TO THE EDGE OF A CLIFF, IT'S WAY TOO LATE TO SAY WHOA.

There are rules to horse ridin', but the horse won't necessarily know 'em.

NEVER DROP YOUR GUN TO HUG A GRIZZLY.

You don't have to
step in a cow pie to know

what shit smells like.

TRUST EVERYBODY
IN THE GAME, BUT
ALWAYS CUT THE CARDS.

It's the work,
not the clock,
that tells you when
it's quittin' time.

IF YOU'RE RIDIN' A HIGH HORSE, THERE AIN'T NO WAY TO GET DOWN OFF IT GRACEFULLY.

A woman's heart
is like a campfire.
If you don't tend
to it regular,
you'll soon lose it.

IF YOU'RE RIDIN' AHEAD
OF THE HERD, TAKE A
LOOK BACK EVERY NOW
AND THEN TO MAKE SURE
IT'S STILL THERE.

IF YOUR KNEES HURT TOO MUCH, YOUR STIRRUPS ARE TOO SHORT. IF YOUR TAIL END HURTS TOO MUCH, YOUR STIRRUPS ARE TOO LONG. IF THEY BOTH HURT, YOUR STIRRUPS ARE JUST RIGHT.

NEVER GO THROUGH A GATE WITHOUT CLOSIN' IT BEHIND YOU.

A GATE ONLY WORKS IF A CORRAL COMES WITH IT.

Always walk tall and
keep your head up—

unless you're walkin'
in a cow pasture.

NO MATTER WHERE
YOU RIDE TO,
★ ★ ★
THAT'S WHERE YOU ARE.

WE MIGHT NOT BE SO BAD OFF IF WE HAD A LITTLE LESS OF EVERYTHING.

WHEN YOU GIVE A LESSON IN
MEANNESS TO A CRITTER OR A
PERSON, DON'T BE SURPRISED
IF THEY LEARN THEIR LESSON.

You will find
it is always
easier to walk if
there is a horse
between your legs.

When your head's in the bear's mouth
is not the time to be smacking him
on the nose and calling him names.

THE QUICKEST WAY TO FEEL RICH IS TO FIGURE OUT WHAT YOU CAN DO WITHOUT.

IF YOU ARE
CARELESS BY
NATURE, YOU
HAVE TO LEARN
TO BE CAREFUL
AS A NECESSITY.

91

If you're gonna
go, go like hell.

★★★

If your mind's
not made up,
don't use your spurs.

Too much debt
doubles the weight on your horse and
puts another in control of the reins.

THE PROBLEM WITH MONEY IS
NOT SO MUCH WHERE IT GOES,
BUT HOW TO GET AHOLD OF IT
TO START WITH.

YOU GENERALLY LEARN
THE VALUE OF MONEY
FROM A LACK OF IT.

MOST BONANZAS ARE JUST HOLES IN THE GROUND OWNED BY BIG BULLSHITTERS.

Entering the
Publishers
Clearinghouse
sweepstakes
every year is not
considered a
well-thought-out
retirement plan.

IF SOMEBODY SAYS YOU RIDE LIKE YOU'RE PART OF THE HORSE . . .

★★★

YOU MIGHT WANNA ASK WHICH PART THEY'RE TALKIN' ABOUT.

THE OLD SAYING THAT FAMILIARITY BREEDS CONTEMPT DOES NOT APPLY TO RATTLESNAKES.

If you're sittin' at
a counter eatin',
leave your hat on.

★ ★ ★

If you're sittin' at a
table, take it off.

A body can
pretend to
care, but they
can't pretend
to be there.

THERE'S NO BETTER FRIEND THAN A HORSE THAT'S SADDLED AND READY TO GO.

IF HORSES AND DOGS AREN'T IN HEAVEN,

I'D JUST AS SOON GO TO TEXAS.

THE WILDEST CRITTERS LIVE IN THE CITY!

IT'S EASY TO SEE THINGS
YOU'RE LOOKIN' FOR.

THE TRICK IS TO SEE THINGS
YOU'RE NOT LOOKIN' FOR.

IT'S RARE TO
FIND A HORSE
THAT EVERYONE
AGREES IS
THE BEST IN
THE HERD.

A LOT OF GOOD LUCK IS UNDESERVED, BUT THEN SO IS A LOT OF BAD LUCK.

★ ★ ★

YOU CAN'T WEIGH
THE FACTS IF
YOU'VE GOT THE
SCALES LOADED
DOWN WITH
YOUR OPINIONS.

SOME THINGS AIN'T FUNNY.

It's hard to keep a secret around the campfire after a hearty meal of pinto whistle berries.

LONESOME BRINGS ON AILMENTS THAT ONLY COMPANY CAN CURE.

SOMETIMES IT
TAKES A LOT
MORE THINKIN'
TO DEAL WITH
CHANGES THAN
TO MAKE THEM.

You can just about always stand
more 'n you think you can.

It don't matter so
much how long a
ride you have, as
how well you ride it.

WHEN IT COMES TO CUSSIN' DON'T SWALLOW YOUR TONGUE;

USE BOTH BARRELS AND AIR OUT YOUR LUNGS.

A MAN WHO WANTS TO LOAN YOU A SLICKER WHEN IT AIN'T RAININ' AIN'T DOIN' MUCH FOR YOU.

REMEMBER, EVEN
A KICK IN THE CABOOSE
IS A STEP FORWARD.

WRONG NO MAN AND WRITE NO WOMAN.

There's only two things you need to be afraid of:

★ ★ ★

a decent woman and bein' left afoot.

ON THE RANGE, AN UNLOCKED RANCH HOUSE IS AN INVITATION TO A WEARY COWBOY TO HELP HIMSELF TO FOOD AND SHELTER. CASH PAYMENT FOR THIS KIND OF HOSPITALITY IS A SERIOUS BREACH OF ETIQUETTE. A NOTE OF THANKS AND PAYMENT IN KIND IS ALL THAT IS EXPECTED.

AVOID FLASHARITY, FOOFARAW, AND FUMADIDDLE IN DRESS, SPEECH, AND CONDUCT.

LEAVE THE PEACOCKING TO THE PEACOCKS.

If you expect
to follow the
trail, you must
do your sleepin'
in the winter.

IN THE MOUNTING OF A HORSE,
THE RIGHT SIDE IS THE WRONG SIDE,
AND THE LEFT SIDE IS THE RIGHT SIDE.
YOUR BACKSIDE IS THE BROAD SIDE,
AND THAT'S THE SIDE YOU SIT ON.

A MIXED HERD OF BOTH SEXES AND ALL AGES IS THE EASIEST KIND TO MANAGE.

A little mud on the carpet from the
boots of honest, working cowboys
is a lot better than a slick-soled
bandbox sitting in a parlor chair.

ANYTIME YOU FIND A LITTLE SHADE,

TAKE IT.

Some waddies take a little time
to work it up and spit it out.

GIVE IT TO 'EM.

Life ain't so short that you can't
take the time to hear a man out.

IF YOU'RE GONNA DRIVE CATTLE
THROUGH TOWN, DO IT ON A SUNDAY.

THERE'S LITTLE TRAFFIC AND PEOPLE
ARE MORE PRAYERFUL AND LESS
DISPOSED TO CUSS AT YOU.

Money may buy
you a dog, but only
love can make
him wag his tail.

A WEEK SPENT
AROUND A
CAMPFIRE
WILL TELL YOU
MORE ABOUT A
MAN THAN A
DECADE SPENT
LIVING NEXT
DOOR TO HIM.

IF YOU LEAD SOMEBODY AROUND BY THE NOSE, IT DON'T SAY MUCH FOR THEM.

IT SAYS EVEN LESS FOR YOU.

Building and fixing fences wouldn't
be so bad if you didn't have to
get off your horse to do it.

The cowboy who
exaggerates too
much soon finds
that everyone
else has left the
campfire.

JUST BECAUSE YOU'RE FOLLOWING
A WELL-MARKED TRAIL DON'T
MEAN THAT WHOEVER MADE IT
KNEW WHERE THEY WERE GOIN'.

THE BEST WAY TO BREAK A BAD HABIT IS TO DROP IT.

If you meet up with an alligator
and he's as scared as you are,

the water won't be fit to drink.

Just because some
yahoo puts Tabasco
in your oatmeal
don't mean you
gotta eat it.

THINGS HAVE A WAY OF WORKIN' OUT IF YOU JUST KEEP YOUR HEAD.

NATURE GAVE US
ALL SOMETHING
TO FALL BACK ON,
AND SOONER OR
LATER WE ALL
LAND FLAT ON IT.

WHEN YOU FORGIVE AND FORGET,

FORGET THAT YOU FORGAVE

WHILE YOU'RE AT IT.

BELIEVE IN MIRACLES, BUT DON'T BET ON 'EM.

DON'T GET MAD AT SOMEBODY
WHO KNOWS MORE 'N YOU DO.

★ ★ ★

IT AIN'T THEIR FAULT.

Never be too quick to criticize yourself.
It's not fair to all your friends and
relatives who are dying to do it for you.

There's no time
to rest when
there's work to be
done. Eat on the
run, forget about
sleep, and change
horses often.

YOU WANNA BE CAREFUL
THAT A FRESHLY BRANDED
CALF AIN'T SUCKIN' AT
THE WRONG COW.

A HORSE AIN'T
TRYIN' TO BE
POLITE WHEN
HE COMES TO
A FENCE AND
LETS YOU GO
OVER FIRST.

IF A COWBOY DROPS BY AROUND
DINNERTIME, IT'S OKAY TO SAY,
"WHAT THE HELL DO YOU WANT?"
BUT YOU STILL HAVE TO INVITE
HIM IN FOR DINNER.

IF YOU'RE GONNA TAKE THE MEASURE OF A MAN,

TAKE THE FULL MEASURE.

Don't take off
too many clothes
when you bed
down on the trail.
You might need to
dress in a hurry.

ALWAYS
REMEMBER, YOUR
HORSE HEARS
AND SMELLS A
WHOLE LOT MORE
'N YOU DO.

NEVER GO TO YOUR ROOM IN THE DAYTIME.

**If you want to liven
up a conversation,**

just say the right thing the wrong way.

WHEN YOU'RE TRYIN' SOMETHIN' NEW, THE FEWER PEOPLE WHO KNOW ABOUT IT, THE BETTER.

Just because a man takes his boots off to go wadin' don't mean he plans to swim the Atlantic.

KICKIN' NEVER GETS YOU NOWHERE,

'LESS YOU'RE A MULE.

The best way
to knock a chip
off a shoulder is
with a friendly
pat on the back.

SEE THE HEAVENS, SMELL THE AIR,
TASTE THE DUST AND THE ALKALI,
HEAR THE WIND AND THE WILD, FEEL
THE MOTION OF YOUR HORSE. . . . ON A
GOOD DAY, THAT'S ALL YOU NEED.

★ ★ ★

ON A BAD DAY, THAT'S ALL YOU NEED.

THERE'S NO PLACE 'ROUND THE CAMPFIRE FOR A QUITTER'S BLANKET.

Only a
buzzard
feeds on his
friends.

DON'T SQUAT WITH YER WITH YER SPURS ON!

NEVER SIT A BARBWIRE FENCE NAKED.

★ ★ ★

WHEN YOU GET BUCKED OFF, THE
EASIEST WAY TO EXPLAIN IT IS TO
SAY YOU DROPPED YOUR HAT AND
GOT OFF IN A HURRY TO GET IT.

A FEW SWEET WORDS AND
A LITTLE BIT OF KINDNESS
CAN COAX THE HOTTEST
IRON OUTTA THE FIRE.

When it's your butt that's
about to go flyin', try to have
more common sense than pride.

Go ahead and choke the horn
and claw the leather.

WHEN YOU THROW YOUR WEIGHT AROUND, BE READY TO HAVE IT THROWN AROUND BY SOMEBODY ELSE.

Most anybody can
be a cowboy,
but it takes a damn
genius to make
any money at it.

WORK LESS AT WORRYING AND MORE AT WORKING.

CONTROL YOUR GENEROSITY WHEN YOU'RE DEALIN' WITH A CHRONIC BORROWER.

There's no such thing as a sure thing.
Let the other fellows
run on the rope if they want to,

but you keep your money in your pocket.

SPEAK YOUR MIND, BUT RIDE A FAST HORSE.

DON'T MAKE A LONG STORY SHORT JUST SO YOU CAN TELL ANOTHER ONE.

The length of
a conversation
don't tell nothin'
about the size of
the intellect.

WHEN YOU'RE PUTTIN' TOGETHER
AN OUTFIT, TAKE YOUR TIME.
WAIT FOR ALL THE LOOSE-LIPPED,
MANICURED COWBOYS TO RUN
THEIR LINE AND WANDER OFF.

THEN MAKE YOUR PICKS FROM
THE WISER HEADS WHO STAYED
AROUND LISTENIN' AND THINKIN'.

There are a lot of reasons to love a horse. Sometimes it's no more than the sweet little way he stepped on some big ass's foot.

DOIN' THINGS THE SMART WAY DOESN'T COST HALF AS MUCH AS DOING 'EM THE STUPID WAY.

No matter where you go or what you do,
keep your saddle and chaps, and always
know where you can get a good ride.

GO AFTER LIFE AS IF IT'S SOMETHING THAT'S GOT TO BE ROPED IN A HURRY BEFORE IT GETS AWAY.

WORKIN' BEHIND A PLOW,
ALL YOU SEE IS A MULE'S HIND END.

WORKIN' FROM THE BACK OF A HORSE,
YOU CAN SEE ACROSS THE COUNTRY
AS FAR AS YOUR EYE IS GOOD.

Solvin' problems is like throwin' cattle.

Dig your heels in on the big ones and catch the little ones 'round the neck.

NEVER RIDE WITH A SADDLE STIFF. HE WILL PREY ON YOUR HONESTY AND LOYALTY.

You cannot improve somebody's part by combing their head with a six-shooter.

HOW LONG YOU LIVE HAS NOTHING TO DO WITH HOW LONG YOU'RE DEAD.

THE BASICS OF ROPING ARE
A SENSE OF RHYTHM, GOOD TIMING,
AND AN EYE FOR DISTANCE.

YOU MIGHT ALSO WANNA KEEP THIS
IN MIND WHEN YOU'RE TWO-STEPPIN'
AROUND THE DANCE FLOOR.

THE ONLY WAY TO DRIVE CATTLE FAST IS SLOWLY.

If you're wonderin' what this ol' world is comin' to, you're in the same shoes as your daddy, your daddy's daddy, and every other daddy that's come down the trail.

NEVER RUN FROM A FIGHT.

IF YOU'RE GONNA GET HIT, IT'S BETTER TO TAKE IT IN THE FRONT THAN IN THE BACK—AND IT LOOKS BETTER.

LETTIN' THE CAT
OUT OF THE BAG IS
A WHOLE LOT EASIER
'N PUTTIN' IT BACK IN.

The best way to set a record is to be a good ways off from any tape measures, scales, or witnesses.

DON'T LET SO MUCH REALITY INTO YOUR LIFE THAT THERE'S NO ROOM LEFT FOR DREAMIN'.

ALWAYS TAKE A GOOD LOOK AT WHAT YOU'RE ABOUT TO EAT.

IT'S NOT SO IMPORTANT TO KNOW WHAT IT IS, BUT IT'S CRITICAL TO KNOW WHAT IT WAS.

A person who
agrees with all your
palaver is either a
fool or he's gettin'
ready to skin ya.

Always carry more 'n one rope.

You might run across
more 'n one rope can handle.

AIN'T NEVER SEEN A WILD CRITTER FEELIN' SORRY FOR ITSELF.

Nothin' keeps
you honest
more than
witnesses.

THE QUICKEST WAY TO DOUBLE YOUR MONEY IS TO FOLD IT OVER AND PUT IT BACK IN YOUR POCKET.

**MOST FOLKS ARE LIKE
A BOB-WIRE FENCE.**

THEY HAVE THEIR GOOD POINTS.

If you want to have
a drink or two,
that's all right—
but don't wear out
your boot soles
on a brass rail.

NEVER MISS A GOOD CHANCE TO SHUT UP.

THE BEST WAY TO KEEP YOUR WORD IS NOT TO GIVE IT FOOLISHLY.

If you own it and run it and have cattle on it—even if you owe the moon on it—it's yours and you're a cattleman. That's what folks will call you.

★ ★ ★

They may call you a good one or a bad one, but they'll call you a cattleman.

IF YOU DRINK TEQUILA, DON'T DIVE OFF THE SIDEWALK. MOST GENERALLY THE WATER IS TOO LOW, AND IN NINE OUT OF TEN TOWNS, THERE IS AT LEAST A $50 FINE FOR IT.

There's a lot
more to ridin' a
horse than just
sittin' in the saddle
and lettin' yer
feet hang down.

PICK THE
RIGHT HORSE
FOR THE JOB.

NOBODY EVER DROWNED HIMSELF IN HIS OWN SWEAT.

No tree is too
big for a short
dog to lift
his leg on.

YOU DON'T NEED DECORATED WORDS
TO MAKE YOUR MEANIN' CLEAR.

SAY IT PLAIN AND SAVE
SOME BREATH FOR BREATHIN'.

TWO DRY LOGS
WILL BURN A
GREEN ONE.

Never lie unless you have to, and if you don't have a damn good lie,

STICK TO THE TRUTH.

If you work for a man, ride for his brand. Treat his cattle as if they were your own.

SOMETIMES COURAGE
TAKES NO MORE THAN
SITTIN' DOWN,
SUCKIN' IT IN,
AND LISTENIN'.

IT'S BETTER TO
SIT ON YOUR
HORSE AND DO
NOTHING THAN
TO WEAR HIM
OUT CHASIN'
SHADOWS.

WHEN YOU GET TO
WHERE YOU'RE
GOIN', THE FIRST
THING TO DO IS
TAKE CARE OF
THE HORSE YOU
RODE IN ON.

Honesty is not somethin' you should flirt with.

You should be married to it.

WET DOGS ARE NEVER WELCOME.

IT DOESN'T MATTER
HOW FAST YOU ARE IF
THE OTHER GUY IS SO
MUCH AS A HAIR FASTER.

Depending on the circumstances,
you can tolerate a certain amount
of slick-eared calf poachin',

but horse stealin' is a hangin' offense.

ADVICE IS LIKE A POT OF CHILI: YOU SHOULD TRY A LITTLE OF IT YOURSELF BEFORE YOU GIVE ANYBODY ELSE A TASTE.

Wear a hat with a brim wide enough to shed sun and rain, fan a campfire, dip water, and whip a fightin' cow in the face.

YOU CAN'T ALWAYS TELL A GUNSLINGER BY THE WAY HE WALKS.

ANY COWBOY
WORTH HIS SALT
HAS A ROPE HAND
THAT ITCHES
CLEAN UP TO HIS
SHOULDER BONE.

WHEN YOU'RE PICKIN' A WORKIN' HORSE, LOOK FOR ONE NAMED SCREWTAIL, STUMP SUCKER, RAT'S ASS, PEARLY GATES, LIVER PILL, OR DARLIN' JILL.

★ ★ ★

LEAVE THE CHAMPIONS AND SILVERS FOR THE SHOW RING.

YOU CAN NEVER STEP IN THE SAME RIVER TWICE.

If you have to count your
chickens before they're hatched,
keep it to yourself.

Nobody gives a damn how many
chickens you're gonna have.

NEVER TAKE ANOTHER MAN'S BET.

HE WOULDN'T OFFER IT IF HE DIDN'T KNOW SOMETHIN' YOU DON'T.

Any time a large
herd moves through
a civilized area,
there's a lot of
shit to clean up.

Coolness and a steady nerve will always beat simple quickness.

Take your time and you'll only need to pull the trigger once.

A CENTER-FIRE RIG WON'T DO ON
STEEP TRAILS. SO WHEN YOU'RE
IN RIMFIRE COUNTRY, ALWAYS
DOUBLE-CINCH YOUR SADDLE.

Never get up before breakfast. If you have to get up before breakfast, EAT BREAKFAST FIRST.

IF YOUR JOB IS TO SHOVEL, AND ALL YOU CAN SEE AHEAD IS DIRT, IT'S TIME TO CHANGE JOBS.

You can always find free cheese in a mousetrap.

If you want to forget all your troubles,
take a little walk in a brand-new
pair of high-heeled ridin' boots.

Comin' as close to the truth as a man can come without actually gettin' there is comin' pretty close, but it still ain't the truth.

IT'S BETTER TO HAVE
A GOOD HORSE FOR A YEAR THAN
AN ASS FOR ALL ITS LIFE.

NEVER JOKE WITH MULES OR COOKS, AS THEY HAVE NO SENSE OF HUMOR.

HOWEVER ONE-SIDED A MAN MAY BE, HE WILL HAVE OTHER SIDES IF YOU LOOK HARD ENOUGH.

Always try to be a
bit nicer than is
called for, but don't
take too much guff.

IT'S BEST TO KEEP YOUR TROUBLES
PRETTY MUCH TO YOURSELF,
'CAUSE HALF THE PEOPLE YOU'D
TELL 'EM TO WON'T GIVE A DAMN,

AND THE OTHER HALF WILL BE
GLAD TO HEAR YOU'VE GOT 'EM.

DON'T ASK FRIENDS FOR MORE 'N THEY WOULD GIVE ON THEIR OWN.

WE COME INTO THIS WORLD
ALL NAKED AND BARE,
WE GO OUT OF THIS WORLD
WE KNOW NOT WHERE.
BUT IF WE HAVE BEEN
GOOD COWBOYS HERE,
WE NEED NOT FEAR WHAT'S
WAITIN' FOR US THERE.

—FAVORITE TOAST OF AB BLOCKER,
LEGENDARY TRAIL DRIVER

Published by
Gibbs Smith
P.O. Box 667
Layton, Utah 84041

Orders: 1.800.835.4993
www.gibbs-smith.com

Designed by Renee Bond
Printed and bound in China

Gibbs Smith books are printed on either recycled, 100% post-consumer
waste, FSC-certified papers or on paper produced from sustainable PEFC-
certified forest-controlled wood source. Learn more at www.pefc.org.

Library of Congress Control Number: 2018951234
ISBN: 978-1-4236-5168-0

23 22   5 4 3 2